English for Mathematics

Linda Glithro
Karen Greenway
Series Editor: Mary Wood

William Collins' dream of knowledge for all began with the publication of his first book in 1819.
A self-educated mill worker, he not only enriched millions of lives, but also founded a flourishing publishing house.
Today, staying true to this spirit, Collins books are packed with inspiration, innovation and practical expertise.
They place you at the centre of a world of possibility and give you exactly what you need to explore it.

Collins. Freedom to teach

HarperCollins*Publishers*
The News Building
1 London Bridge Street
London SE1 9GF

**Browse the complete Collins catalogue at
www.collins.co.uk**

First edition 2016

10 9 8 7 6 5 4 3 2 1

© HarperCollins*Publishers* 2016

ISBN 978-0-00-813571-3

Collins® is a registered trademark of HarperCollins Publishers Limited

www.collins.co.uk

A catalogue record for this book is available from the British Library

Written by Karen Greenway and Linda Glithro
Series edited by Mary Wood
Commissioned and conceptualised by Karen Jamieson
Editorial management by Mike Appleton
Copyedited by Tanya Solomons
Proofread by Cassie Fox
Artwork and typesetting by QBS
Cover design by Amparo Barrera and Ken Vail Graphic Design
Printed by CPI Group (UK) Ltd, Croydon, CR0 4YY

Introduction

This series of books is aimed at non-native English speakers who attend English language mathematics lessons in primary school. The books aim to support those who find the language used in the lesson unfamiliar and challenging.

Some of the language of mathematics is rarely used outside the classroom, so may be unfamiliar to those students who don't speak English as their first language. In some cases words and phrases can have a different meaning in the mathematics classroom to their meaning in common usage. This can lead to confusion and frustration, and can hinder progress.

The *English for Mathematics* series aims to teach students the language used for mathematics taught in upper primary school. Key words and language structures are explained, using diagrams and illustrations to aid understanding. The 'Wise Owl' gives tips and hints on how to use the language, allowing learners to check their understanding. Carefully graded activities linked to the topic and the focus vocabulary give opportunities to practise using the language.

Each of the 36 units includes notes to teachers or parents, which give ideas for how to present the language and topics to learners. The books can be used in class alongside the main textbook, or at home for further practice and reinforcement.

The clear, easy-to-use layout, and the appealing and helpful pictures and diagrams, will help de-mystify the English of Mathematics.

Mary Wood, Series Editor

English for Mathematics: Book B
Linda Glithro and Karen Greenway

Contents

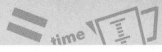

Partitioning numbers

Read it!

Key words: **digit, place value, thousand, zero, place value holder, partition, ten thousand (10 000)**

The position of a **digit** in a number gives its **place value** or size.

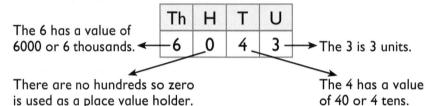

The 6 has a value of 6000 or 6 thousands. ← 6 0 4 3 → The 3 is 3 units.

There are no hundreds so zero is used as a place value holder.

The 4 has a value of 40 or 4 tens.

The 6 has a place value of 6000 or 6 thousands.
There are no hundreds so **zero** is used as a **place value holder**.
The 4 is 40 or 4 tens.
The 3 is 3 units.

Partitioning a number breaks it into parts.
Example:
Instruction: Partition 3125.
Answer: $3125 = 3000 + 100 + 20 + 5$

Remember – each place is 10 times the value of the place to its right.

ten thousand

TTh	Th	H	T	U
1	0	0	0	0

$\times 10 \times 10 \times 10 \times 10$

1 ten thousand
= 10 × 1 thousand

Language focus!

Everyday meaning of **digit**: a finger, thumb or toe

Mathematical meaning of **digit**: any of the numerals 0, 1, 2, 3, 4, 5, 6, 7, 8 or 9

Think about it!

1. **Describe the place value of the 5 in these numbers.**

   4**5**81 _____ **5**109 _____ 128**5** _____

2. **Finish partitioning these numbers.**

   (a) $8452 = 8000 +$ _____ $+$ _____ $+ 2$

   (b) $6703 =$ _____ $+ 700 +$ _____

Practise it!

1. (a) Write these numbers in figures.

One thousand nine hundred and sixteen _____

Three thousand four hundred and two _____

Six thousand and eighty four _____

(b) Write these numbers in words.

5739 _____

7094 _____

2810 _____

2. (a) Partition these numbers.

4759 = _____ + _____ + _____ + _____

3602 = _____ + _____ + _____

8015 = _____

(b) Put these partitioned numbers back together.

2000 + 800 + 40 + 3 = _____

7000 + 300 + 4 = _____

9000 + 80 = _____

3. Here are four digit cards.

Using all four of these cards what is …

(a) the largest number you can make? _____

(b) the largest even number you can make? _____

(c) the smallest number you can make? _____

(b) the smallest odd number you can make? _____

Teachers' and parents' note

Look for numbers to read, write and discuss in everyday life. Remind students to read numbers from the left. You start with the digit that has the largest place value. 2609 is two thousand six hundred and nine. Make sure that they remember to use zero as a place value holder. Four thousand and sixty is 4060 and ten thousand is 10 000.

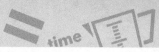

Decimal numbers

Read it!

Key words: decimal, decimal point, tenth, hundredth, decimal place

A **decimal** (or decimal number) is a number containing a whole number part and a fraction part.

The **decimal point** separates the whole number part from the fraction.

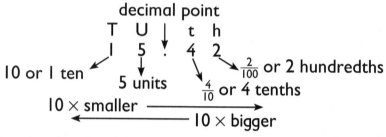

decimal point

T U ↓ t h

1 5 . 4 2

10 or 1 ten

5 units

$\frac{4}{10}$ or 4 tenths

$\frac{2}{100}$ or 2 hundredths

10 × smaller ———→

←——— 10 × bigger

Example: | H T U • t h | represents the number 412.61

This number has 4 hundreds, 1 ten, 2 units, 6 tenths and 1 hundredth.

Language focus!

The first **decimal place** shows the number of **tenths** (t).

The second **decimal place** shows the number of **hundredths** (h).

A centimetre is one hundredth of a metre.
1 metre + 25 centimetres
= 1.25 metres
1.25 m = 125 cm

Think about it!

1. **What is the value of the seven in these numbers?**

   (a) 3.72 _____   (b) 7.43 _____   (c) 1.87 _____

2. **Change these amounts from metres to centimetres.**

   (a) 2.65 m = _____   (b) 0.90 m = _____   (c) 1.04 m = _____

Practise it!

1.

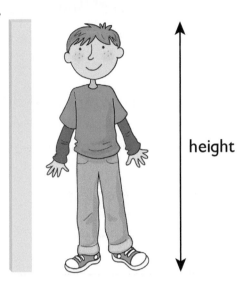

height

Ali is 115 cm tall, which is equivalent to 1.15 m.

What is the height of these children in metres?

(a) Anton 124 cm = _____

(b) Bruno 131 cm = _____

(c) Conrad 109 cm = _____

2. Complete the table for the number 184.39.

The first row has been done for you.

tens	8
units	
hundreds	
tenths	
hundredths	

3. Put these lengths in order, starting with the largest.

1.99 m   655 cm   5.45 m   200 cm

_____

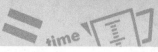

Rounding numbers

> Key words: round (a number to ...), between (half way between), closer to, closest to

Rounding a number makes a simpler number. It is less accurate but easier to use. The number is still close to what it was.

To round to the nearest 10, round down a units digit of 4 or less, and round up a units digit of 5 or more.

347 is **between** 340 and 350 but **is closest to** 350.
347 is 350 when rounded to the nearest 10.

To round to the nearest 100, round down a tens digit of 4 or less, and round up a tens digit of 5 or more.

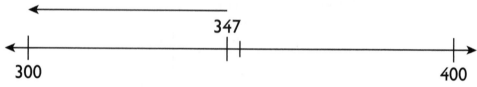

Example:
Question: What is 347 rounded to the nearest 100? (Look at the tens digit.)
Answer: 300 (347 is rounded down to 300 because 4 tens are nearer to 300 than 400.)

Language focus!
Between, half way between, closer to

The whole numbers 71, 72, 73, 74, 75, 76, 77, 78 and 79 are between 70 and 80

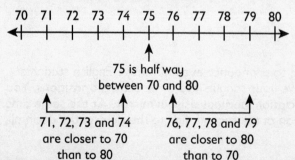

70 71 72 73 74 75 76 77 78 79 80

75 is half way
between 70 and 80

71, 72, 73 and 74
are closer to 70
than to 80

76, 77, 78 and 79
are closer to 80
than to 70

> 5 is exactly in the middle, but the rule is that the digit 5 is always **rounded up**.

Think about it!

1. Round these numbers to the nearest 10.

(a) 432 _____ (b) 567 _____ (c) 408 _____

2. Round these numbers to the nearest 100.

(a) 762 _____ (b) 639 _____ (c) 527 _____

Practise it!

1. Tick (✓) the number that is closest to 500.

538   485   5050   490   515

2. Complete the table.

	Rounded to the nearest 10	Rounded to the nearest 100
493		
3465		
752		
6056		

3. Mia is rounding numbers to the nearest 10.

Her answer is 650.

List **all** the whole numbers she could use.

_____

Teachers' and parents' note

Ask individual students to explain to you how they would round a number to the nearest 10 (100). Remind them that they can use a number line to make it clear. 'Teaching' another person is an excellent way to develop understanding.

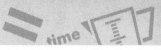

Comparing numbers

Read it!

Key words: compare, size, number line, order, greater than (>), less than (<)

You **compare** numbers by looking at the difference in their size, for example 125 is less than 152.

To **compare** and **order** 4-digit numbers, look at the thousands digit, then the hundreds digit, then the tens digit and finally the units digit.

Example: Here are four numbers: 5251   6782   5673   5256

Instruction: Arrange the numbers in order of size starting with the smallest number. Estimate the positions of the smallest and largest numbers on a 0–10 000 number line.

Answer: 5251, 5256, 5673, 6782

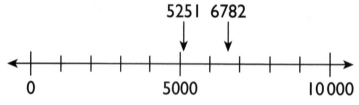

5251 6782

0–10000 number line marked in multiples of 1000

Language focus!

equal	=	$3 + 6 = 4 + 5$
greater than	>	$3 + 6 > 4 + 3$
less than	<	$3 + 6 < 4 + 9$

$8 > 6$ This says: 'Eight is **greater than** six.'

$6 < 8$ This says: 'Six is **less than** eight.'

We can order numbers in a list or show the order using the < and > signs.
$5673 > 5256 > 5251$
or
$5251 < 5256 < 5673$

Think about it!

Write > or < in the box to make these statements correct.

(a) 9032 ☐ 8965

(b) 4512 ☐ 4152

Practise it!

1. Write > or < in each circle.
Then write a whole number that comes in between each pair.

(a) 3569 ◯ 3659 _____

(b) 7111 ◯ 799 _____

(c) 2099 ◯ 2101 _____

(d) 6407 ◯ 6079 _____

2. Match each letter to the correct number.

5723 is _____ 5140 is _____ 5981 is _____ 5369 is _____

3. Here are 4 digit cards.

(a) Write all the 4-digit numbers greater than 7000 that can be made using all 4 cards.

_____

_____

(b) Put the numbers you made in order of size starting with the smallest.

_____

_____

Teachers' and parents' note

Look for opportunities to compare numbers. Ask questions like: Were there more people at the football match this month or last? Which river is the longest? Which village has the greater population?

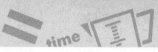

Negative numbers

Read it!

Key words: **negative number, positive number, zero, temperature**

A **negative number** is less than **zero** (0). It is written with a minus sign.
A **positive number** is greater than zero.

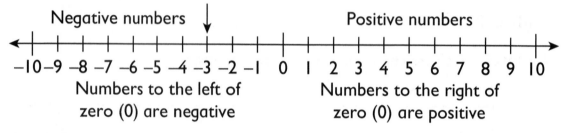

Negative numbers ↓   Positive numbers

−10 −9 −8 −7 −6 −5 −4 −3 −2 −1   0   1   2   3   4   5   6   7   8   9   10

Numbers to the left of   Numbers to the right of
zero (0) are negative   zero (0) are positive

A thermometer is an instrument for measuring **temperature**.
Temperatures are measured in degrees Celsius (°C).

Example:
Question: Look at the number line. Which number is shown
by the arrow?
Answer: −3

Language focus!

A negative number is written with a minus sign in front, for example −7.
Read this as 'negative seven'.

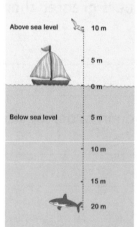

Above sea level   10 m

5 m

0 m

Below sea level   5 m

10 m

15 m

20 m

Sea level is 0 m. Negative numbers describe depths below sea level. Positive numbers give heights above sea level.

Think about it!

Look at the number line on the image above.

(a) What is the position of the seagull?

(b) What is the position of the shark?

Practise it!

1. Here is a temperature scale.

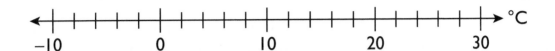

The temperature is 1° below freezing on a cold day.
Mark with an arrow (↑) the position of this temperature on the scale.

2. Here are some temperatures:

−4°C   −2°C   1°C   −8°C

(a) Which is the coldest temperature?

_____

(b) Which is the warmest temperature?

_____

(c) Write the temperatures in order of size starting with the warmest.

_____

3. What temperature is shown on these thermometers?

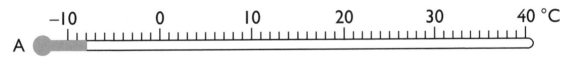

A

B

(a) A is _____ °C

(b) B is _____ °C

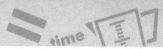

Odd and even numbers

Read it!

Key words: even, odd, next, general statement, counter example

Even numbers are multiples of 2. They end in 0, 2, 4, 6 or 8.

Odd numbers have a remainder of 1 when they are divided by 2.

multiple of 2   multiple of 2   multiple of 2

O E O E O E O E
101 102 103 104 105 106 107 108····

O stands for an odd number
E stands for an even number

Example: ... 52, 54, 56, _____, _____, _____
Instruction: Write the **next** three even numbers.
Answer: 58, 60, 62

Language focus!

Definition	Example
A **general statement** is a statement of a rule that is always true.	When I add two odd numbers, the answer is always even.
A **counter example** is an example that proves a general statement is wrong.	General statement: 'When I add an odd number and an even number the answer is even.' This statement can be proved to be incorrect by this counter example: 3 + 4 = 7 This answer is odd.

We can use examples to illustrate a general statement such as 'The sum of two odd numbers is even'.
We can use O to stand for odd and E to stand for even and write this as O + O = E.
Example: 3 + 5 = 8 (3 and 5 are odd, 8 is even)

Think about it!

1. **Write an example to illustrate the general statement E + E = E**

2. **Write a counter example to show that this general statement is false.**
   E − O = E _____

Practise it!

1. Here is a Venn diagram for sorting numbers.

Write each number in the correct place in the diagram.

135   6   122   94   271   108

Find and write one more number for each area.

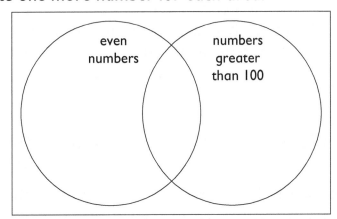

2. Here are four digit cards.

Use three or four cards each time to make the following numbers:

4   3   8   2

(a) a 3-digit even number greater than 400 _____

(b) a 4-digit odd number greater than 4000 _____

(c) a 3-digit odd number less than 300 _____

(d) a 4-digit odd number less than 3000 _____

3. Bruno says: "I take away an odd number from an odd number and my answer is an odd number."

(a) Find a counter example to show that Bruno is wrong.

_____

(b) Write the correct general statement.

_____

_____

Teachers' and parents' note

Encourage students to establish general statements for adding and subtracting two numbers. If necessary, help them to develop a coding system, for example E + E = E, O + O = E, O + E = O and E + O = O where E = any even number and O = any odd number.

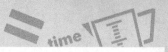

Number sequences

Read it!

Key words: sequence, rule, term, continue, count on, count back

A **sequence** is a list of numbers in order that follow a numerical **rule**.
Here is the sequence of odd numbers. Each number is a **term** in the sequence.

| 1 | 3 | 5 | 7 | 9 | 11 | ... |

1st term   2nd term   3rd term   The three dots show that the sequence **continues** indefinitely.

The **rule** explains how to find the next **term**. The rule for this sequence is 'add 2'.

Example: Look at this sequence: 64, 60, 56, 52, 48, _____, _____, ...
Question: What are the next two terms? What is the rule?
Answer: 44, 40   The rule is 'subtract 4'.

Language focus!
Count on, count back

Numerical sequences count on or count back in ones, tens, hundreds or any other number.

Example:
A 'count on 50' sequence:
$60 \xrightarrow{+50} 110 \xrightarrow{+50} 160 \xrightarrow{+50} 210 \xrightarrow{+50} 260$

To find the rule for a sequence, find the difference between consecutive terms (terms that are next to each other).
Example:

     −25   −25   −25   −25   −25

| 225 | 200 | 175 | 150 | 125 | 100 |

The rule is 'subtract 25'.

Think about it!

1. **Fill in the missing numbers in these sequences.**
   (a) 0, 30, 60, 90, _____, _____, ...

   (b) 1, 10, 19, 28, _____, _____, ...

2. **Write the rule for each sequence.**
   (a) 140, 120, 100, 80, 60, 40   The rule is _____.
   (b) 4, 10, 16, 22, 28, 34   The rule is _____.

6

Practise it!

1. Write the first five terms of each sequence. Explain the rule.

(a) The first term is 10. Now count on in 100s.

———, ———, ———, ———, ———

_____

(b) The first term is 100. Now count back in 10s.

———, ———, ———, ———, ———

_____

(c) The first term is 5. Now count on in 5s.

———, ———, ———, ———, ———

_____

(d) The first term is 10 000. Now count back in 1000s.

————, ————, ————, ————, ————

_____

2. Each sequence starts with 0. Write the first five terms.

(a) The rule is add 50.   ———, ———, ———, ———, ———

(b) The rule is add 13.   ———, ———, ———, ———, ———

(c) The rule is subtract 2.   ———, ———, ———, ———, ———

(d) The rule is add 99.   ———, ———, ———, ———, ———

3. The rule for this sequence of numbers is 'add four each time'.

1,   5,   9,   13,   17,   21,   25 …

The sequence continues in the same way.

Circle the number that does **not** belong to the sequence?

33   49   44   29

Teachers' and parents' note

Discuss with students how times tables are numerical sequences, for example 4, 8, 12, 16, … The rule is add 4. Some events, like the Olympic Games, follow sequences. The Olympic Games takes place every four years so the rule is add 4 to the year. Try to find other examples of sequences.

Equivalent fractions

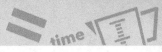

Read it!

Key words: equivalent fraction, numerator, denominator, part
(equal parts)

Equivalent fractions are the same size.
Equivalent fractions such as $\frac{1}{5}$ and $\frac{2}{10}$
look different but are the same size.

$$\frac{1}{5} = \frac{2}{10}$$

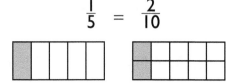

Example:
Instruction: Write two fractions that are equivalent to $\frac{1}{2}$.
Answer: $\frac{2}{4}$ and $\frac{3}{6}$ (other answers are possible)

Language focus!

$\frac{3}{4}$

The **numerator** (top number)
shows how many equal parts are
in the fraction.

The **denominator** (bottom number)
shows how many equal parts the
whole number is divided into.

A fraction wall shows
fractions that are
equivalent. You can use
the wall to compare
and order fractions.

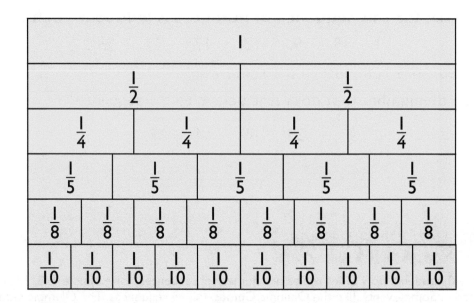

Think about it!

Complete these equivalent fractions.

(a) $\frac{1}{2} = \frac{\square}{8}$

(b) $\frac{3}{4} = \frac{\square}{8}$

(c) $\frac{1}{2} = \frac{\square}{10}$

Practise it!

1. Write the equivalent fractions shown in these diagrams.

(a)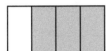

____ = ____

(b)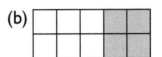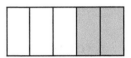

____ = ____

(c)

____ = ____

2. There are three fractions in each set. Circle the two fractions that are equivalent.

(a) $\frac{4}{8}$ $\qquad$ $\frac{6}{10}$ $\qquad$ $\frac{1}{2}$

(b) $\frac{7}{10}$ $\qquad$ $\frac{3}{4}$ $\qquad$ $\frac{6}{8}$

(c) $\frac{8}{10}$ $\qquad$ $\frac{3}{4}$ $\qquad$ $\frac{4}{5}$

3. Complete each number statement using =, > or <. Use the fraction wall to help you.

(a) $\frac{1}{2}$ $\square$ $\frac{5}{8}$

(b) $\frac{1}{4}$ $\square$ $\frac{2}{8}$

(c) $\frac{9}{10}$ $\square$ $\frac{4}{5}$

(d) $\frac{4}{10}$ $\square$ $\frac{1}{2}$

Teachers' and parents' note

Understanding fractions is a really important aspect of mathematical development. You should try to give students lots of practical experience using concrete materials. There are many games and visual materials available to help consolidate understanding.

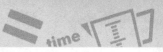

Ordering fractions

Read it!

Key words: compare, numerator, in order, denominator, number line

To **compare** fractions change them so they have the same denominator.
Look at the size of the numerators to **order** them.

To **compare** $\frac{3}{8}$ and $\frac{1}{2}$, write both fractions with the same denominator.
$\frac{1}{2} = \frac{4}{8}$ $\frac{3}{8} < \frac{4}{8}$ so $\frac{3}{8} < \frac{1}{2}$

Example: Put the fractions $\frac{6}{10}$, $\frac{1}{2}$ and $\frac{3}{10}$ **in order** on a 0–1 number line.
Answer:

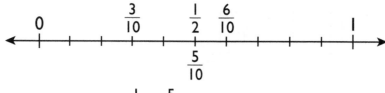

I know that $\frac{1}{2} = \frac{5}{10}$

Language focus!

Order

Everyday meaning: **an order** is a command or strong request

Definition in mathematics: **in order** means to arrange things by size

A common instruction is: Put these numbers **in order**.

Using a number line is a good way to compare and order fractions. You change all the fractions to the same denominator so you can see the fraction sizes clearly.

Think about it!

1. Write $>$, $<$ or $=$ between each pair.

   (a) $\frac{1}{4}$ ____ $\frac{3}{8}$ (b) $\frac{4}{8}$ ____ $\frac{2}{4}$ (c) $\frac{7}{8}$ ____ $\frac{3}{4}$

2. Put the fractions $\frac{3}{10}$, $\frac{1}{2}$ and $\frac{1}{5}$ in order on a 0–1 number line.

Practise it!

1. Write the three fractions in order, starting with the smallest.

   (a) $\frac{3}{4}$, $\frac{5}{8}$, $\frac{1}{2}$ _____

   (b) $\frac{2}{5}$, $\frac{3}{10}$, $\frac{1}{2}$ _____

2. These questions are about number lines.

   (a) Write the missing fraction on the number line.

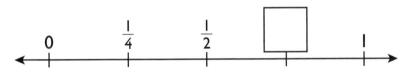

   (b) Write the fractions $\frac{9}{10}$, $\frac{1}{2}$, $\frac{4}{5}$ and $\frac{7}{10}$ on the number line.

   (c) Show the fractions $\frac{5}{8}$, $\frac{1}{2}$, $\frac{1}{4}$ and $\frac{3}{8}$ on a blank number line.

3. Circle the fractions that are greater than one half.

   $\frac{3}{10}$ $\frac{5}{8}$ $\frac{6}{10}$ $\frac{1}{8}$

Teachers' and parents' note

Many students experience difficulties with fractions, possibly because of an over-reliance on the 'part of a whole' model. Ensure they understand that fractions and mixed numbers can be represented as a position on a number line by providing suitable examples.

Mixed numbers

Read it!

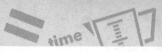

Key words: mixed number, order, compare, number line

A **mixed number** is a number that is a whole number and a fraction.

whole number ⟶ $2\frac{3}{4}$ ⟵ fraction

$2\frac{3}{4}$ is read as 'two **and** three quarters'.

A number line can be used to **order** and **compare** numbers.
$1\frac{1}{2}$, $2\frac{3}{4}$, $3\frac{1}{4}$ are placed **in order**, starting with the smallest number.

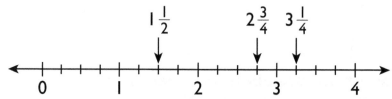

The number sentence $3\frac{1}{4} > 2\frac{3}{4}$ **compares** $3\frac{1}{4}$ with $2\frac{3}{4}$ showing that $3\frac{1}{4}$ is greater than $2\frac{3}{4}$.

Example:
Question: Use < or > to compare $1\frac{1}{2}$ and $2\frac{3}{4}$.
Answer: $1\frac{1}{2} < 2\frac{3}{4}$

Language focus!

mix	put together
mixed	assorted, different, varied

Mixed numbers come between whole numbers on a number line. $7\frac{1}{8}$ is between 7 and 8, closer to 7.
$7\frac{3}{4}$ is also between 7 and 8, closer to 8.

Think about it!

1. **Write these mixed numbers.**

   (a) five and seven eighths _____

   (b) four and three tenths _____

2. **Write the children's ages in order, youngest to oldest.**

   $7\frac{3}{4}$, $8\frac{1}{4}$, 8, $7\frac{1}{2}$, $8\frac{1}{2}$ _____

Practise it!

1. Write the mixed numbers shown by the letters on the number line.

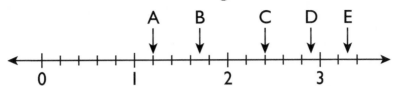

A = _____ B = _____ C = _____ D = _____ E = _____

2. Show each pair of mixed numbers on the number line. Circle the one that is closer to 2.

(a) $1\frac{3}{5}$ and $2\frac{3}{10}$

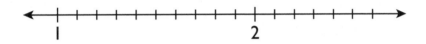

(b) $1\frac{7}{8}$ and $2\frac{1}{4}$

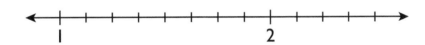

3. Here is part of a number line. Write the two missing mixed numbers.

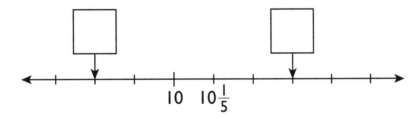

Teachers' and parents' note

Encourage students to use a number line to visualise mixed numbers. Draw a blank section of number line with the appropriate whole numbers marked. Find the halfway point between the whole numbers to show $\frac{1}{2}$ and finally further sub-divide each half into quarters or tenths according to the question.

Addition

Read it!

Key words: calculate, add, plus, sum, more than, total, number line, partition

The addition calculation 347 + 289 can be presented using different words.

> **Calculate** 347 + 289.

> **Add** 347 and 289.

> 347 **plus** 289

> Find the **sum** of 347 and 289.

> What is 347 **more than** 289?

> Find the **total** of 347 and 289.

Example: 347 + 289 can be worked out using a number line or by partitioning.

(a) Using a number line

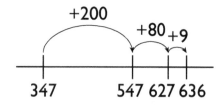

(b) Using partitioning

$$
\begin{aligned}
347 &= 300 + 40 + 7 \\
289 &= 200 + 80 + 9 \\
\hline
&\;\;\;500 + 120 + 16 \\
&= 600 + 30 + 6 \\
&= 636
\end{aligned}
$$

347 + 289 = 636

Language focus!
Partition

A partition can be placed across a room to divide it into two smaller parts.

It can be moved to a different position.

You can partition numbers in different ways:

436 = 400 + 30 + 6

or 400 + 20 + 16

or 420 + 16 …

> Look how the numbers 347 and 289 are partitioned into hundreds, tens and units in the example. This makes the addition easier to do.

Think about it!

Look at the two ways of adding 347 and 289.
How do the 'jumps' on the number line relate to the partitioning method?

_____

Practise it!

Here are three different questions. Each one starts with a **command word** that tells you what to do.

1. Calculate 495 + 678.

> **Calculate** means work out the answer.

2. Complete the diagram so the three numbers on each line total 1000.

> **Complete** means finish the puzzle.

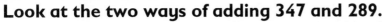

368 — 241

521

463

3. Use the digits 2, 3, 4, 5, 6 and 7 to complete the calculation.

☐☐☐ + ☐☐☐ = 900

> **Use** means you must use the given information as part of the question.

Teachers' and parents' note

The aim is for students to use mental methods for addition whenever possible. For calculations they cannot do in their head, however, they need to be able to use an efficient written method, such as the partitioning method shown. When they are ready to understand the column method, they can use that. The column method is compact and efficient and can be used with numbers of any size, including decimals.

Subtraction

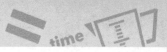

Read it!

Key words: subtract, minus, difference, take away, count back, leave (left)

The subtraction calculation 527 − 348 can be presented using different words.

Subtract 348 from 527.

527 **minus** 348.

Find the **difference** between 348 and 527.

Take away 348 from 527.

Use a number line to **count back** 348 from 527.

Example: 527 − 348 can be worked out using a number line or by partitioning.

(a) Using a number line

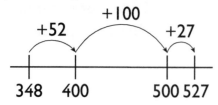

+100

+52   +27

348   400   500 527

Add the jumps:

52 + 100 + 27 = 179

You can count on from the smaller number or count back from the larger number.

(b) Using partitioning

$527 = 500 + 20 + 7$

527 = 400 + 110 + 17 ← Partitioning
348 = 300 + 40 + 8   the number
―――――――――   in a different
       100 + 70 + 9   way means
    = 179   you can do the
                            subtraction
                            easily.

Language focus!

Left

Everyday meaning	(1) The past of *leave*, for example: *The children left school after lunch.* (2) The side opposite right (left hand, turn left)
Mathematical meaning	The amount remaining after a subtraction.

You can check your answer to a subtraction calculation by adding your answer to the number you subtracted.

Think about it!

Take 189 away from 342 using a number line and by partitioning.

Check that you get the same answer each time.

Practise it!

Here are three different questions. Look carefully at the words in bold and the speech bubbles.

1. **A family plans a road trip of 500 miles. On the first day they travel 158 miles. What distance is left to drive?**

2. **On Friday Jamil scores 612 points in a computer game. This is 146 points more than his score on Thursday. Find his score for Thursday.**

   > The word 'more' sounds like an addition sum – and it often is. But in this question 'more than' requires a subtraction.

3. **Jasper thinks of a 3-digit number and adds 150. The answer is 358. What is Jasper's number?**

   > Think about this question carefully. It is not an addition question.

Teachers' and parents' note

Encourage students to get into the habit of estimating the answer before they begin each calculation. It will flag up if it is possible to carry out the calculation mentally. If their answer differs greatly from the estimate, it will show that there is probably an error in the calculation.

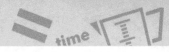

Multiplication and division

Read it!

Key words: multiple, inverse

Multiples of any number can be divided exactly by that number.

2, 4, 6, 8 and 10 are all **multiples** of 2.

An **inverse** operation reverses the effect of another operation. Multiplication and division are **inverse** operations.

To multiply by 10 move the digits 1 place to the left.

H	T	U
	×10	3
×10	3	0
3	0	0

$3 \times 10 = 30$
$30 \times 10 = 300$
$3 \times 100 = 300$

To divide by 10 move the digits 1 place to the right.

H	T	U
3	0	0
÷10	3	0
	÷10	3

$300 \div 10 = 30$
$30 \div 10 = 3$
$300 \div 100 = 3$

Example:
Question: Which operation is the inverse of subtraction?
Answer: Addition

Language focus!

Inverse operations have the opposite effect.

add 3	subtract 3
multiply by 10	divide by 10
double	halve
turn 90° clockwise	turn 90° anticlockwise
go left 5 steps	go right 5 steps

You can use inverse operations to check an answer.
Question: 75×3
Answer: 225
Check: $225 \div 3 = 75$

Think about it!

Complete the calculations and check the answer using an inverse calculation.

Question 1: 306×10
Answer:
Check:

Question 2 : $4800 \div 100$
Answer:
Check:

Practise it!

1. **Missing number problems are often solved using inverses.**

   Example: $3 \times \boxed{} = 30$

   The answer is found by calculating $30 \div 3$.

   Now try these:

   (a) $6080 \div \boxed{} = 608$

   (b) $\boxed{} \times 10 = 1600$

   (c) $\boxed{} \div 100 = 750$

2. **Find the missing numbers.**

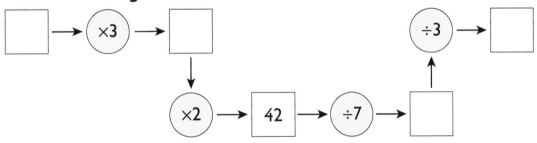

3. **True or false? Circle the correct answer.**

   (a) 2005 is a multiple of 100.   True / False

   (b) Multiples of 10 are also multiples of 5.   True / False

   (c) 5600 is a multiple of 5, 10 and 100.   True / False

   (d) 7030 is a multiple of 100.   True / False

Teachers' and parents' note

Encourage students to make up puzzles like the one in question 2. They can then swap them with their friends and discuss how they solve them. Discourage students from saying that you add two zeros to multiply by 10 or take away two zeros to divide. This approach will cause problems when they meet decimals numbers.

Mental strategies

Key words: recall, derive, pairs, total

It is possible to **recall** some facts instantly, for example $3 + 7 = 10$.
Knowing one fact can help you work out or **derive** (work out) other related
facts, for example $10 - 3 = 7$ or $13 + 7 = 20$ or $1003 + 7 = 1010$
Over time, you will recall facts that you once had to derive.

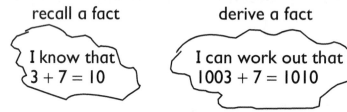

recall a fact   derive a fact

I know that $3 + 7 = 10$ I can work out that $1003 + 7 = 1010$

Finding **pairs** of numbers is a useful skill in mental mathematics.

Example:

Pairs of numbers that total 100

multiples of 10,
for example $30 + 70$

not multiples of 10,
for example $29 + 71$

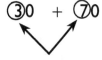

$\textcircled{3}0 \ + \ \textcircled{7}0$

sum of tens digits is 10

$\textcircled{2}9 \ + \ \textcircled{7}1$ sum of tens digits is 9
and
sum of units digits is 10

Pairs of multiples of 50 that **total 1000** include $350 + 650$ and $250 + 750$.

Language focus!

Derive

This is not a common word in English but it is a useful one in mathematics. It means to find out by reasoning.

When you add several small numbers, look for pairs that equal 10 or 20 and add these first.

$4 + 18 + 2 + 16 = 40$

6

Think about it!

Here is a number fact: 35 + 65 = 100
Use this fact to **derive** other facts.

(a) $65 + \boxed{} = 100$

(b) $\boxed{} - 35 = 65$

(c) $350 + 650 = \boxed{}$

(d) $1000 - 350 = \boxed{}$

Practise it!

1. **Find pairs of numbers in the box that total 100. Write them on the lines below.**

   Which number does not have a pair? _____

33	63	74	62	17
51	14	2	45	52
21	38	67	42	91
9	55	49	86	37
26	83	48	98	79

   _____ _____ _____

   _____ _____ _____

   _____ _____ _____

   _____ _____ _____

2. **Derive facts to continue these patterns.**

   $50 + 950 = 1000$ $1000 - 50 = 950$

   $100 + \boxed{} = 1000$ $1000 - \boxed{} = 900$

   $150 + \boxed{} = 1000$ $1000 - \boxed{} = 850$

   $\boxed{} + \boxed{} = 1000$ $1000 - \boxed{} = \boxed{}$

   $\boxed{} + \boxed{} = 1000$ $\boxed{} - \boxed{} = \boxed{}$

3. **Continue these patterns.**

   $21 - 9 = 12$ $10 - 7 = 3$
   $31 - 19 =$ $100 - 70 =$
   $41 - 29 =$ $1000 - 700 =$
   $51 - 39 =$ $10\,000 - 7000 =$

Teachers' and parents' note

Games and number square activities can help students to develop and recognise patterns so that the knowledge becomes fully mastered, for example: $12 - 3 = 9$, $22 - 13 = 9$, $32 - 23 = 9$.

Multiplication

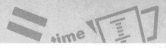

Read it!

Key words: product, multiply, grid method, times

To find the **product** of two numbers, multiply them together.

The **grid method** is a method of multiplication where numbers are partitioned in a grid.

The calculation 78×6 can be presented in different ways:
- **multiply** 78 by 6
- **times** 78 by 6
- 78 **lots of** 6
- 78 **groups of** 6
- find the **product** of 78 and 6

Example:

Instruction: Multiply 78 by 6 using the grid method.

Answer:

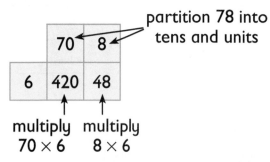

partition 78 into tens and units

multiply 70×6 multiply 8×6

add the answers together

$420 + 48 = 468$

Language focus!

Product

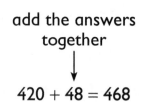

We can multiply numbers in any order so $3 \times 25 = 25 \times 3$ and $2 \times 16 \times 10 = 10 \times 16 \times 2$.

Everyday meaning	A manufactured article.
Mathematical meaning	The answer when two or more numbers are multiplied together.

Think about it!

Calculate the answers.

(a) Multiply 45 by 2 _____

(b) Find the product of 25 and 4. _____

Practise it!

1. Find the answers to these multiplication questions.

   (a) Find the product of 9 and 4. _____

   (b) 6 multiplied by 8. _____

   (c) 4 times 7. _____

   (d) Find 7 lots of 3. _____

2. Use the grid method to answer these multiplication questions.

   (a) 47×6

   (b) 79×9

3. In this number wall, the product of two numbers gives the number above.

12

2	6

12

↑

product of 2 and 6

Use the same rule to work out the missing numbers in this number wall.

25	20

	4

Teachers' and parents' note

Provide students with activities to help them learn times tables. You could use grids like these:

×	2	4	6
3			
4			
5			

×	4		10
	20	15	
	8		20
6		18	

Division

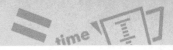

Read it!

> Key words: divide by, divide into, share (between), remainder, half (halve)

When you **divide** something in mathematics you split it into equal pieces or groups.

The calculation 97 ÷ 5 can be presented in different ways:
- **divide** 97 **by** 5
- **divide** 5 **into** 97
- **share** 97 equally **between** 5

Example: Calculate 97 ÷ 5.

(a)   Using a number line

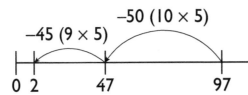

(b)   Repeated subtraction

```
    97
  − 50      10 × 5
    47
  − 45       9 × 5
     2
```

After the division, 2 is left over. We say 'the remainder is 2' and write this as r 2.

Answer: 19 r 2

Language focus!

Half, halve

Verb: When you **halve** something you divide it into two equal parts or reduce something by half.

Noun: The plural of the noun **half** is **halves**.

You can partition a 2-digit number to help you find half of it.

| Find half of 68 | $\frac{1}{2}$ of 68 |

60 + 8
30   4
30 + 4 = 34

Think about it!

1. **Complete the number sentences.**

   (a) 10 divided into 50 is _____.

   (b) 10 divided by 5 is _____.

2. **Write the remainder for these division calculations.**

   (a) 44 divided by 5 = 8 r _____

   (b) 84 divided by 9 = 9 r _____

Practise it!

1. Find the answer to each of these division questions.

(a) 14 oranges are shared equally between 7 people.

How many oranges does each person get? _____

(b) How many tens are there in seventy? _____

(c) 49 divided by 7. _____

(d) Divide 35 by 5. _____

2. Choose a suitable method to work these out.

(a) 43 divided by 5.

(b) Divide 68 by 6.

3. Pedro has 48 triangular tiles.

He uses them to make a quadrilateral like this.

How many quadrilaterals can Pedro make?

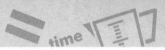

Division problems

Read it!

Key words: context, round up, round down

Word problems are set in a **context**.
The **context** is the setting for a question.

$$27 \div 5 = 5 \text{ r } 2$$

In a problem it depends on the context whether you **round** the answer **up** or **down**.

Round the answer down

A box holds 5 toys.
How many boxes can you fill with 27 toys?

You can fill 5 boxes.

You will have 2 toys left over.

Round the answer up

27 people want to visit a castle by taxi. Each taxi holds 5 people. How many taxis do they need?

They need 6 taxis.

2 people would be left behind if there were only 5 taxis.

Language focus!
Round up, round down

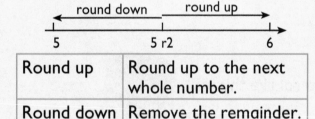

Round up	Round up to the next whole number.
Round down	Remove the remainder.

To solve a question set in context:
• Find the key words in the problem.
• Decide which operation(s) to use.
• Complete the calculations.
• Check the answer makes sense.

Think about it!

1. Round these calculations down.

(a) $74 \div 6 =$ _____ r _____ $74 \div 6$ rounded down is _____.

(b) $83 \div 5 =$ _____ r _____ $83 \div 5$ rounded down is _____.

2. Round these calculations up.

(a) $75 \div 9 =$ _____ r _____ $75 \div 9$ rounded up is _____.

(b) $58 \div 3 =$ _____ r _____ $58 \div 3$ rounded up is _____.

Practise it!

1. **Work out these division calculations. The key words are underlined in part (a).**

   (a) 80 eggs are packed in boxes. Each box holds 6 eggs. How many full boxes are there?

       There are _____ full boxes.

   (b) There are 69 guests at a dinner. Each table can seat 6 people. How many tables are needed?

       You need _____ tables.

   (c) Tickets cost $9. Eva has $70. How many tickets can she buy? ($ stands for dollar.)

       Eva can buy _____ tickets.

2. **Use this division calculation, 46 ÷ 6, to write:**

   (a) a word problem where you need to **round** the answer **up**.

   _____

   _____

   (b) a word problem where you need to **round** the answer **down**.

   _____

   _____

Polygons

Read it!

Key words: polygon, quadrilateral, pentagon, hexagon, heptagon, octagon, regular, irregular

A **polygon** is a 2D shape with 3 or more straight sides.
Polygons with different numbers of sides have different names.

   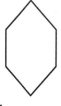

| triangle | quadrilateral | pentagon | hexagon | heptagon | octagon |
| (3 sides) | (4 sides) | (5 sides) | (6 sides) | (7 sides) | (8 sides) |

Example:
Instruction: Name this shape.
Answer: A heptagon.

Language focus!
Prefixes for numbers

Prefix	Number
tri	3
quad	4
pent	5
hex	6
hept	7
oct	8

In **regular** shapes all the sides are the same length and all the angles are equal. Shapes that do not have all their sides the same length or all their angles equal are called **irregular** shapes.

regular   irregular
pentagon   pentagon

Think about it!

Draw a ring around the shapes that are polygons.

Practise it!

1. Put these polygons in order using the number of sides.

Start with the smallest.

| heptagon | octagon | quadrilateral | pentagon |

_____   _____   _____   _____

smallest   largest

2. Use the triangular grid to draw a regular hexagon and an irregular heptagon.

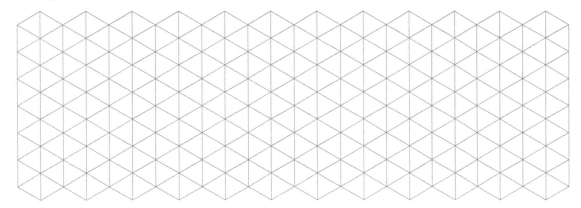

3. Draw lines to join each shape to the correct place in the Carroll diagram.

	regular shapes	not regular shapes
polygons		
not polygons		

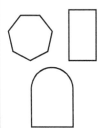

Quadrilaterals

Read it!

Key words: 2-dimensional, quadrilateral, side, vertex (vertices), square, rectangle, kite, adjacent, opposite, pinboard

A **2-dimensional** or 2D shape is a shape with 2 dimensions (such as length and width) but no thickness.

sides   vertices

A **quadrilateral** is a 2D shape with 4 straight **sides** and 4 **vertices**. Some quadrilaterals have special names.

square	rectangle	kite
4 equal sides 4 right angles	opposite sides are equal 4 right angles	2 pairs of adjacent, equal sides

Language focus!

adjacent next to		The sides are next to each other. They meet at a point.
opposite facing		Opposite sides face each other.

A **pinboard** is a board with nails equally spaced on a square grid. Elastic bands are used to make shapes. The shapes can be drawn on spotty paper like the ones above. Right angles and sides of equal length are easy to identify.

Think about it!

Use the spotty paper to draw 3 different quadrilaterals.

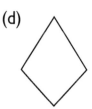
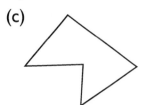

Practise it!

1. Put a tick in the shapes that are quadrilaterals.

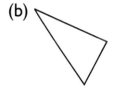

  (a)   (b)   (c)   (d)

2. This pattern is made up of four different types of quadrilateral.

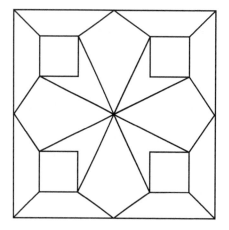

Colour each type of quadrilateral in a different colour.

Write the names of the quadrilaterals that have special names.

_____

_____

3. Luis makes some quadrilaterals using 2 triangles like this one.

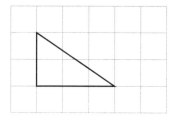

He records the shapes on a squared grid. Show what 2 of his shapes could look like on this grid.

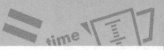

Symmetrical shapes

Read it!

Key words: **symmetrical, line of symmetry, reflection, mirror line, polygon, regular**

A **symmetrical** shape has at least one line of symmetry.

A **line of symmetry** cuts the shape into two identical pieces where one half is the **reflection** of the other.

When the line of symmetry is shown on a shape it is sometimes labelled as the **mirror line**.

Example:

Question: Is a kite a symmetrical shape?

Answer: Yes, it has one line of symmetry.

Some shapes have more than one line of symmetry.

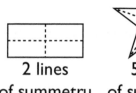

mirror line

mirror line

mirror line

mirror line

2 lines
of symmetry

5 lines
of symmetry

Language focus!

Focus words

Polygons are 2D shapes with 3 or more straight sides. Regular shapes have all sides the same length and all angles equal.

A regular polygon has the same number of lines of symmetry as the number of sides.

4 sides
4 lines
of symmetry

5 sides
5 lines
of symmetry

6 sides
6 lines
of symmetry

Think about it!

Draw all of the lines of symmetry on these shapes.

 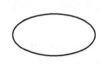 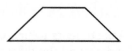

Practise it!

1. How many lines of symmetry does each shape have?

Write the number below the shape.

(a)

(b)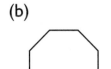

(c)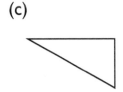

(d)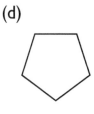

_____   _____   _____   _____

2. These patterns have lines of symmetry.

Draw all the lines of symmetry in the patterns.

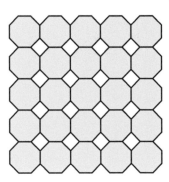 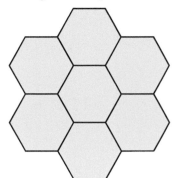 

3. Use the square grid to draw a hexagon with exactly 2 lines of symmetry and a quadrilateral with only 1 line of symmetry.

Teachers' and parents' note

Look for examples of symmetrical shapes and patterns in the real world, such as honeycombs, starfish and orange segments. Give students practical experience of creating symmetrical shapes by asking them to cut shapes from a folded piece of paper.

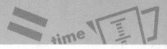

3D shapes

Read it!

Key words: 3-dimensional, solid, cuboid, prism, pyramid, tetrahedron, face, edge, vertex, base, cube

A **3-dimensional shape** or 3D shape is a shape with three dimensions such as length, width and height. It is sometimes called a **solid** shape.

Some 3D shapes have special names:

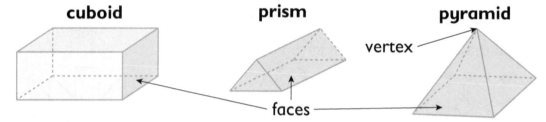

cuboid   prism   pyramid

vertex

faces

Example:

Question: A shape has 1 hexagonal face and 6 triangular faces. What is it called?

Answer: A hexagonal pyramid.

A pyramid that has 4 equal triangular faces is called a **tetrahedron**.

Language focus!

The shape of the base gives a pyramid its name. The shape of the end faces gives a prism its name.

A cuboid with 6 identical faces is called a cube. Cuboids and cubes are special types of prisms.

Think about it!

Rosa says: "I am thinking about a shape. It has 4 triangular faces. The triangles are all the same size."

(a) Name Rosa's shape. _____

(b) Think of a hexagonal prism. How would you describe it to someone?

_____

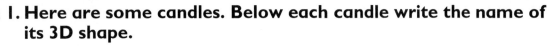
Practise it!

1. **Here are some candles. Below each candle write the name of its 3D shape.**

(a)

(b)

(c)

(d)

_____   _____   _____   _____

2. **Some 3D shapes have been drawn on the dotted grid. The first one is complete (you cannot see any of the internal lines). Complete the other two shapes in the same way.**

square based pyramid   cube   hexagonal prism

3. **Complete the table about different types of pyramids.**

Name of shape	Number of edges	Number of faces	Number of vertices
tetrahedron			
square based pyramid	8		
pentagonal pyramid		6	
hexagonal pyramid			7

Write about any patterns that you can see in the information?

_____

_____

Teachers' and parents' note

Give students experience of 3D shapes using models. Ask them to count the faces, edges and vertices, and discuss the names of the faces. Play a game using a bag, like in the Think about it! question. Can a student describe the shape well enough for another student to name it? If possible, let them build the shapes from click-together shapes, or straws and connectors.

Nets

Read it!

Key words: net, pyramid, prism, cuboid

A net is a set of 2D shapes that can be folded to make a 3D shape.

This net will fold to give a square based pyramid.

Example:

Question: Which shape will this net make?

Answer: A pentagonal prism.

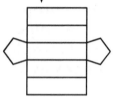

The shape of the base of a pyramid or the end face of a prism gives the 3D shape its name.

Language focus!

Shape of base or end face	Pyramid	Prism
square	square based pyramid	cuboid
pentagon	pentagonal pyramid	pentagonal prism
hexagon	hexagonal pyramid	hexagonal prism

All the faces of a pyramid are triangles except the base. All the faces of a prism are rectangles except the end faces.

Think about it!

Tick the nets that will fold to make a triangular prism.

(a)

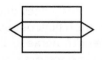

(b)

(c)

(d)

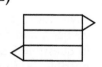

Practise it!

1. Draw lines to match each net to the correct 3D shape.

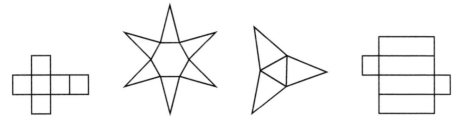

| hexagonal pyramid | cuboid | cube | triangular pyramid |

2. Lia is drawing the net of a hexagonal prism.

Here is her drawing. Two faces are missing.

Sketch the shapes in the correct places to complete the net.

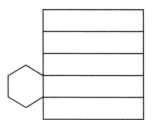

3. Use the triangular grid to draw the net of a tetrahedron.

49

Using grids

Read it!

Key words: grid, row, column, horizontal, vertical, axis (axes), position

A **grid** is made of rows and columns of squares.

The rows are **horizontal**.
The columns are **vertical**.

A grid can have a **pair of axes** that are labelled with letters and numbers.
The letters are on the horizontal axis and the numbers are on the vertical axis.

The letters and numbers give the **position** of an object on the grid.

Example: Look at the grid.
Instruction: Give the position of the bee.
Answer: C1

vertical axis

← horizontal axis

Language focus!

Horizontal	The horizon is horizontal.	A horizontal line runs across the page, from left to right.
Vertical	In an upright position.	A vertical line runs up and down the page.

When you give the location of an object on the grid, always read along the horizontal axis → first then up the vertical axis ↑. The answer should be a letter followed by a number.

Think about it!

Here is a square grid showing 2D shapes.

(a) Where is the hexagon? _____

(b) Which shape is in E1? _____

(c) Give the position of the triangle. _____

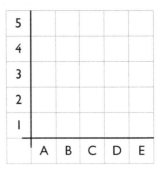

Practise it!

1. Here is a grid labelled with letters and numbers.

(a) Write T in C5.

(b) Write K in A2.

(c) Write E in D3.

(d) Write I in B4.

What shape does this spell? _____

2. Here is another blank grid.

(a) Shade these squares on the grid.

    B3   C6   A4   D3

(b) Shading one more square would make a symmetrical pattern.

Give the position of this square. _____

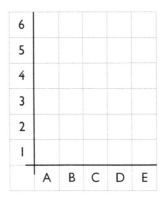

Teachers' and parents' note

Look at examples of local maps and plans that use a grid labelled in this way. Find the positions of buildings or other objects.

51

Giving directions

Read it!

Key words: directions, left, right, up, down, route

Directions are instructions that tell you how to get from one place to another on a map or plan. To give directions on a grid we use the instructions **left** and **right** to move horizontally, and **up** or **down** to move vertically.

3	greenhouse		potatoes			apples				
2	path									
1	peas		carrots			beans				
	A	B	C	D	E	F	G	H	I	J	K

← left   right →

up
down

Example: Look at the plan of the garden.
Question: How would you go from the greenhouse to the carrots?
Answer: 1 square right and 2 squares down (as shown by the red lines).

On a map or plan, the directions to go from one place to another is called a **route**.

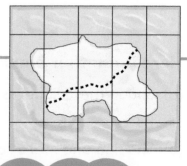

Language focus!
Opposites

up	down
left	right
forwards	backwards

In real life we move forwards and backwards around a room but on a grid this becomes up and down.

Think about it!

Look at the plan of the garden.

1. Raj is standing in H1. He moves 2 squares up and 1 square left. Which vegetable area is he standing in now? _____

2. Fatima is standing in square J3 and she wants to go to the greenhouse. Write directions to take her to the greenhouse.

_____

Practise it!

I. Here is a map of the village where Julia and Salima live. X marks a door.

(a) The red line shows Salima's route to school. She goes up 1 square and left 3 squares. Complete the directions for Salima's route to school.

_____

_____

_____

(b) Draw Julia's route from the shop to her house on the plan. Write directions to show how to get there.

_____

_____

2. Here is a plan of a school. X marks a door.

(a) Joseph is at the door to classroom 1. How would he get to the door into the playground?

_____

_____

_____

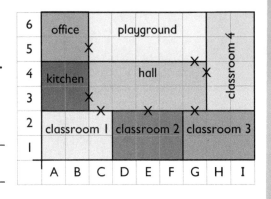

(b) Mr Tsu is at the door to classroom 3. How would he get to the office?

_____

_____

Teachers' and parents' note

Ask the students to move about the room following directions, for example: 4 steps forwards, turn right, forwards 3 steps. Compare this with giving directions on a paper plan of the room. How would the vocabulary change?

Angles

Read it!

Key words: angle, degree, right angle, clockwise, anticlockwise

An **angle** measures how far an object turns.
The amount of turn is measured in **degrees**.

a whole turn	a half turn or straight line

 or   or

measures 360°   4 right angles   measures 180°   2 right angles

Example: Look at the diagram above.
Question: How many degrees does 1 right angle measure?
Answer: 90°

An angle can turn

clockwise   anticlockwise

in the same direction   in the opposite direction
as the hands of a clock   to the hands of a clock

Language focus!
Degree

A unit for measuring the size of an angle. It is marked with the symbol °.
A unit used in temperature measurements: °C (Celsius) or °F (Fahrenheit).
An award on completion of a university course.

We can use arrows to show which way we are turning – clockwise or anticlockwise. On an angle diagram we show this with a curve.

Think about it!

How far has each arrow turned? Write 90°, 180° or 360°.

(a)   (b) 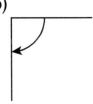 (c) 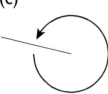 (d)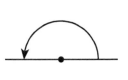

_____   _____   _____   _____

Practise it!

1. **Put these angles in order, starting with the smallest. Write each letter in the correct space below.**

(a)   (b)   (c)  (d)

_____   _____   _____   _____

smallest   largest

2. **This is the control on a cooker.**
   The dial turns clockwise and anticlockwise.

   (a) The cooker is off.
       Luis turns the dial 90° clockwise.
       Which number does it point to? _____

   (b) The dial is on 2.
       Luis turns it off.
       How far did the switch turn? _____

   (c) The dial is on 3.
       Luis wants to turn the cooker off.
       Give two ways that he could do this? _____

Teachers' and parents' note

Ask students to find examples of other things that turn such as a compass, cogs, switches or a steering wheel. Give them practical experience of turning through angles: play 'Simon says' with 90°, 180°, 360°, clockwise and anticlockwise.

Length

Read it!

Key words: kilometres, metres, centimetres, millimetres

Length is the measurement of how far it is from one end of an object to the other or the distance between two points.

It is measured in kilometres, metres, centimetres or millimetres.

Example: Look at this diagram.
Question: Measure the length of the square in millimetres.
Answer: 15 mm

Width and height are measured in the same way as length.

A rectangle has 2 dimensions.

A cuboid has 3 dimensions.

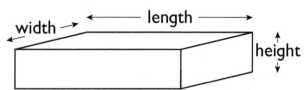

Language focus!

How wide? → How much wider?
How far?   → How much further?
How near? → How much nearer?

The names of the measurements are usually shortened in mathematical questions to make them easier to use: kilometres = km, metres = m, centimetres = cm and millimetres = mm.

Think about it!

Which units would you use to measure these items?

Write mm, cm, m or km.

(a) The height of a tree _____

(b) The width of a ribbon _____

(c) The distance between two towns _____

(d) The length of a pencil _____

Practise it!

1. Measure these lines using cm and mm.

For example: 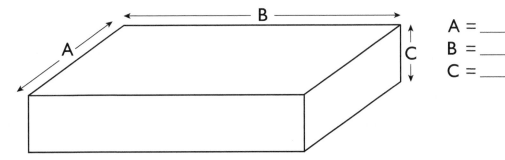 This line is 2 cm and 7 mm long.

A _____

B _____

C _____

D _____

2. Here is a diagram of a cuboid. Measure the length of sides A, B and C in mm.

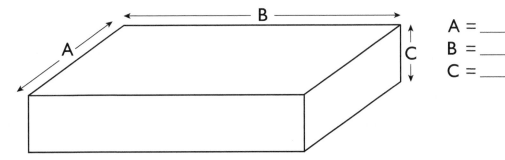

A = _____
B = _____
C = _____

3. Solve these word problems.

(a) The distance from Abbotsville to Brimstone is 153 km.
Heidi drives 75 km then stops for a break.
How much further does she have to go? _____

(b) Here is the plan of a garden.
Jamil wants to put a fence around the perimeter.

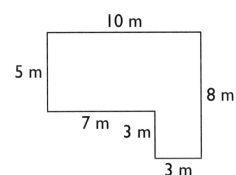

(i) How long is the perimeter of the garden? _____

(ii) Fence panels measure 2 m each. How many fence panels will he need? _____

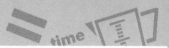

Capacity and mass

Read it!

Key words: litres, millilitres, grams, kilograms

Capacity is used to measure the amount held by a container. We use capacity to measure liquids (like water or juice). It is measured in litres and millilitres.

We weigh items to find their mass. We use mass to measure solids (like butter, flour or rice). It is measured in kilograms and grams.

Example: Flora is baking bread. She measures out the flour and water.

Question: What is the mass of the flour? How much water did she use?
Answer: Flour = 450 g
Water = 300 ml

Capacity is measured with a measuring jug or beaker.	Mass is measured with different types of scales.

Language focus!
Prefixes

kilo: means a thousand in Greek so 1 kilogram means 1000 grams

milli: means a thousand in Latin but in measures is used to mean one thousandth

Remember
1 kilogram = 1000 grams
so 1 kg = 1000 g.
1 litre = 1000 millilitres
so 1 l = 1000 ml.

Think about it!

Which units would you use to measure these items?
Write millilitres, litres, grams or kilograms.

(a)
(b)
(c)
(d)

Practise it!

1. Here is a jug of orange juice.

(a) Omar fills a glass with juice from the jug.
How much juice is left in the jug?

_____

(b) What is the capacity of the glass?

_____

(c) Omar fills another identical glass.
Mark the level of juice left in the jug.

2. Valentina places four identical tins of beans and six 100 g weights on a balance. They balance exactly.

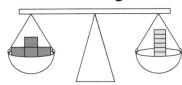

(a) What is the mass of two tins of beans? _____

(b) What is the mass of 1 tin of beans? _____

(c) Emma takes 1 tin off the balance.
Draw the pans on this
diagram to show what
the balance would
look like now.

Teachers' and parents' note

Look at familiar packets, bottles and jars – are they measured using mass or capacity? Use these to ensure that students are clear about the difference between the measures of liquids and dry goods.

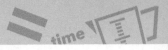

12-hour clock

Key words: day, hour, minute, second, midnight, noon,
analogue clock, digital clock

A **day** is divided into 24 **hours**.
Each **hour** is divided into 60 **minutes**.
An analogue clock times 12 hours.
Each time appears twice in a day.

4 o'clock   4 o'clock
in the morning in the afternoon

The 12 hours from **midnight** to **noon** are **a.m.** times.
The 12 hours from **noon** to **midnight** are **p.m.** times.

Example:
Question: Is 6:00 p.m. in the morning or the afternoon?
Answer: Afternoon.

We can say a time in different ways: **digital clock**   **analogue clock**
- as it is shown on the digital clock: two forty-seven

- as the number of minutes **past** the hour:
  forty seven minutes past two

- as the number of minutes **to** (or before the
  next hour): thirteen minutes to three

Describing time

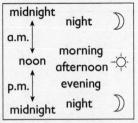

Morning describes a.m. times.
Afternoon and evening describe
p.m. times. Night can be either
a.m. or p.m. depending on whether
it is before or after midnight – the
middle of the night.

Write morning, afternoon or evening under these 12-hour clock times.

(a) 4:37 p.m.   (b) 2:14 a.m.   (c) 8:42 p.m.   (d) 9:29 a.m.

_____   _____   _____   _____

Practise it!

1. Here are some analogue clocks.
Write the equivalent digital time under each clock.

(a)

(b)

(c)

(d)

_____   _____   _____   _____

2. Draw a line to join each time to the correct label – a.m. or p.m.

| One ten in the afternoon |
| Half past seven in the morning |
| Nineteen minutes past two at night |
| Twenty to eight in the evening |

a.m.

p.m.

3. Answer the following questions.
Remember to put a.m. or p.m. in your answers.
Here is the clock in Milly's classroom.

(a) Milly's maths lesson finished 35 minutes ago. What time did it finish?

_____

(b) In 10 minutes it will be lunch time. What time does Milly go to lunch?

_____

(c) Lunch lasts for 45 minutes. What time will it end?

_____

Teachers' and parents' note

Use images of events taking place at different times of the day to show students the difference between a.m. and p.m. times, especially at night. Ensure that students understand the different ways of saying times, for example 6:53 can be six fifty-three, fifty-three minutes past six or seven minutes to eight. Remind them that the hour hand on the clock continues to move very slowly throughout the hour and only points exactly to the number on the hour itself.

Timetables

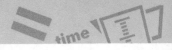

Read it!

Key words: timetable, arrive, depart, calendar, date

A **timetable** is a chart showing information about the time that things happen.

A bus or train timetable shows when a vehicle **arrives** or **departs** each day.

A school timetable shows what happens on each day of the week.

Bus Station	7:10	7:40	8:10
High Street	7:15	7:45	8:15
School Lane	7:18	7:48	8:18
Park Road	7:24	7:54	8:24
College Way	7:30	8:00	8:30

	M	T	W	Th	F
9–10	Maths	Geog.	Hist.	Eng.	Maths
10–11	Eng.	Maths	Maths	Sci.	Eng.
11–12	Sci.	Eng.	ICT	Maths	P.E.
12–1	Hist.	Geog.	D.T.	Art	Sci.

Example: Look at the school timetable.
Question: What subject do the students have on Wednesday at 10 o'clock?
Answer: Maths

A **calendar** is a special type of timetable that shows the day and month.
This is called the **date**.

day — Tuesday
5th
month — May

days of the week

Language focus!

arrive = reach a point on a journey
depart = leave a point on a journey

Remember – there are 7 days in a week and 52 weeks in a year. There are 365 days in a normal year and 366 days in a leap year.

Think about it!

Look at the bus timetable at the top of the page.

(a) What time does the second bus arrive at School Lane? _____

(b) How long does it take to travel between High Street and

Park Road? _____

Practise it!

1. Here is the timetable for the local swimming pool.

Days of the week	Times
Monday, Tuesday and Friday	7:30 a.m. to 7:30 p.m.
Wednesday and Thursday	noon to 7:30 p.m.
Saturday and Sunday	11:00 a.m. to 6:30 p.m.

(a) What time does the pool open on Thursdays? _____

(b) How long is the pool open for on Saturdays? _____

(c) Ahmed arrives at the pool at 6:15 p.m. on Monday.

How long does he have to swim? _____

2. Here is part of a local train timetable for Sydney, Australia.

Penrith	10:29	10:54	11:09	11:24
Emu Plains	10:42	10:57	11:12	11:27
Lapstone	-	11:03	-	11:33
Glenbrook	10:51	11:07	11:21	11:33
Blaxland	10:57	11:13	11:27	11:37
Warrimoo	-	11:16	-	11:43
Valley Heights	-	11:20	-	11:50
Springwood	11:07	11:25	11:37	11:55

(a) When does the second train arrive in Warrimoo? _____

(b) How long does the 11:24 take to get from Emu Plains to Blaxland?

_____

(c) How do you know that the 11:09 does not stop at Valley Heights?

_____

Teachers' and parents' note

Use examples of local bus or train timetables to give students the opportunity to read real information. Show students other types of timetables and calendars to broaden their experience. Remind students of the rhyme for remembering the number of days in each month: *Thirty days has September, April, June and November. All the rest have thirty-one except February alone, which has twenty-eight days clear and twenty-nine in a leap year.*

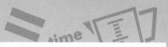

Perimeter

Read it!

Key words: perimeter, length, width

The **perimeter** is the distance all around the edge of a shape.
To find the perimeter of a rectangle, measure the **length** and the **width**.

Add the measurements together:
6 cm + 3 cm + 6 cm + 3 cm = 18 cm

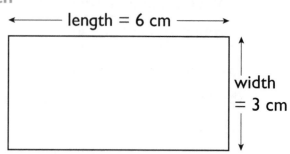

length = 6 cm

width = 3 cm

You can find the perimeter of a rectangle using doubling.

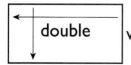

length = 6 cm

double   width = 3 cm

Not drawn to scale

length = 6 cm

+

width = 3 cm

Double the length: 6 cm × 2 = 12 cm
Double the width: 3 cm × 2 = 6 cm
This gives a total of 18 cm

Add the length and the width:
6 cm + 3 cm = 9 cm
Double the results: 9 cm × 2 = 18 cm

Language focus!
Focus words

The word perimeter contains the word rim. Rim means edge. This can help you to remember what to measure.

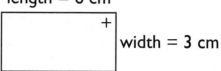

In the diagrams above, the rectangles are labelled '**Not drawn to scale**'. This means that the diagram represents a real rectangle that would measure 6 cm by 3 cm, but this takes up less space on the page.

Think about it!

Calculate the perimeter of each rectangle.

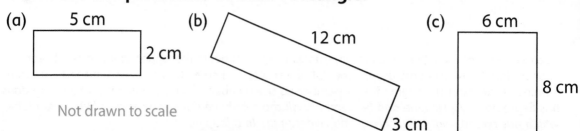

(a)   5 cm

2 cm

Not drawn to scale

(b)   12 cm

3 cm

(c)   6 cm

8 cm

Practise it!

1. **Measure the length and width of these rectangles. Then work out the perimeter.**

(a)   (b)

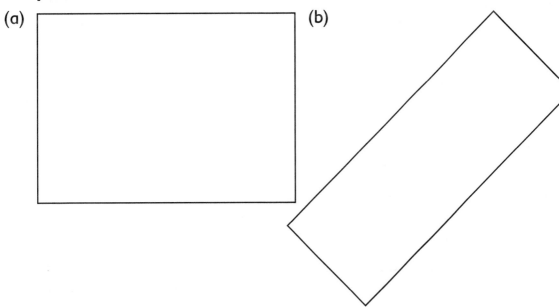

2. (a) A square has a perimeter of 16 cm.
      What is the length of each side?

_____

   (b) Use the centimetre square grid to draw 2 rectangles with the same perimeter as the square.

Teachers' and parents' note

Remind students that as they draw around a plastic or cardboard shape they are tracing the perimeter. Some students confuse area and perimeter so it important to emphasise the link between perimeter and tracing around a shape.

Area

Read it!

Key words: area, square centimetre, square metre

Area measures the space inside a 2D shape.
It is measured using squares.

To find the area of a shape,
count the squares inside it.

area

Example: Look at the diagram above.
Question: What is the area of the rectangle?
Answer: 15 squares.

Small areas such as a photograph
or a tile are measured in square
centimetres.
This is written cm^2.

Large areas such as a field or football
pitch are measured in square metres.
This is written m^2.

   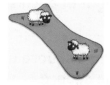 

Language focus!

We say square centimetres, but
it is abbreviated to cm^2.
We say square metres, but it is
abbreviated to m^2.

Often area and perimeter are
linked in questions. Remember: area
measures the space inside a shape.
Perimeter measures the distance
around the edge of the shape.

Think about it!

Find the area of each of these shapes.

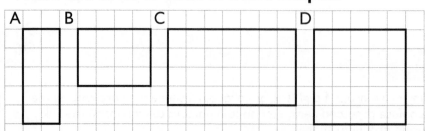

A = _____ squares

B = _____ squares

C = _____ squares

D = _____ squares

Practise it!

1. Use the square grid to draw 2 rectangles that each have an area of 12 cm².

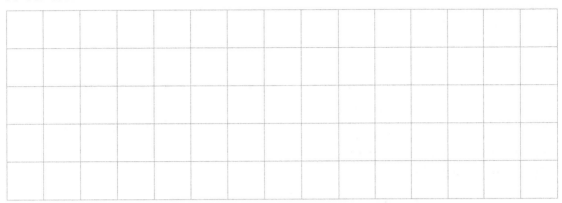

2. Find the area of each rectangle. Remember to write cm².

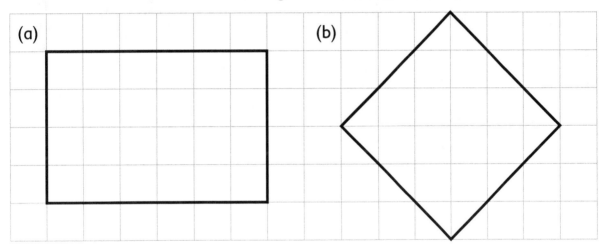

(a)

(b)

3. Vijay says: "The rectangle I have drawn has an area of 18 cm². It is 6 cm long." How wide is Vijay's rectangle? Use the grid to experiment.

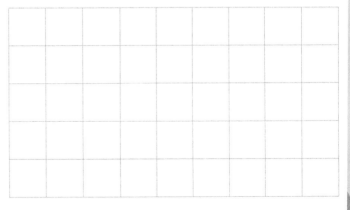

Teachers' and parents' note

Ask students to experiment with other items to find the area of a rectangle (counters, coins). Discuss why squares are the best way to fill the shapes exactly. Give them practical experience of drawing different rectangles that cover the same area.

Using tables

Read it!

Key words: table, row, column, Carroll diagram, sort

A **table** is a grid of **rows** and **columns** that shows information clearly.

Example: Look at the table.
Question: How tall is Everest?
Answer: 8848 metres

A **Carroll diagram** is a table with 2 rows and 2 columns not including the labels.
It is used to **sort** information using different properties.

Mountain	Height in metres	Continent
Aconcagua	6960	South America
Elbrus	5642	Europe
Everest	8848	Asia
Kilimanjaro	5895	Africa
Mckinley	6168	North America

columns

labels

	Multiples of 4	Not multiples of 4
Odd numbers		1 3 5 7 9 11
Not odd numbers	4 12 8	2 10 6

rows

Language focus!

Rows are the sections of the table that go across the page.

Columns are the sections of the table that go up and down the page.

The labels on the rows and columns of the Carroll diagram must be:
• has the property
• does **not** have the property.

Think about it!

Look at the Carroll diagram above.

(a) Write 28, 17 and 34 in the correct places in the diagram.

(b) Why is one box of the diagram empty?

Practise it!

1. Here is a table about dinosaurs.

Name of dinosaur	Length (m)	Height (cm)	Mass (kg)
Stegosaurus	9.1	340	2722
Triceratops	7.9	290	6350
T. Rex	15.2	700	6350
Velociraptor	1.8	60	113

(a) How long is the Triceratops? _____

(b) Which dinosaur has a mass of 2722 kg? _____

(c) Which dinosaur is the shortest? _____

(d) How much taller than the Stegosaurus is the T. Rex? _____

2. Write the names of these shapes in the correct place on the Carroll diagram.

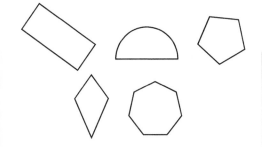

	Polygon	Not a polygon
Quadrilateral		
Not a quadrilateral		

3. 40 young people go to an activity centre.

They can choose either climbing or swimming.

Use this information to help you complete the table.

- There are 24 boys at the activity centre.

- 11 girls go swimming.

	Climbing	Swimming	Total
Boys	15		
Girls			
Total			40

Teachers' and parents' note

Ask students to look for tables in books and magazines and discuss the information found in them. Give students practical experience of sorting shapes and number cards in a Carroll diagram.

Collecting data

Read it!

Key words: **data, tally chart, frequency table, tally marks**

Data is a set of information that is needed to answer a question. It is collected by asking questions, observing or measuring.

Ten boys are asked what their favourite sport is. They answer: football, cricket, swimming, football, cricket, football, football, cricket, football, football.

The data can be organised in a **tally chart** or a **frequency table**.

Tally chart to show favourite sports

Sport	Tally	Total
cricket	|||	3
football	|||||	6
swimming			1

← tally marks

Frequency table to show favourite sports

Sport	Frequency
cricket	3
football	6
swimming	1

Example: Use the tally chart to answer this question.
Question: Which sport is most popular?
Answer: Football

Language focus!

most popular or most common
= largest amount shown

least popular or least common
= smallest amount shown

A tally mark is made for each object counted.

1	2	3	4	5	6	7
I	II	III	IIII	ЖНҬ	ЖНҬ I	ЖНҬ II

The fifth mark is made across the other four to make it easier to see the total.

Think about it!

Look at the data in the charts above.

(a) Which is the least common sport? _____

(b) How many more boys prefer football to cricket? _____

Practise it!

1. **Here is a tally chart to show the vehicles passing a school one morning. Some of the tally marks and totals are missing. Use the information you have to complete the chart.**

Type of vehicle	Tally	Total
bicycle	ⅣⅢ Ⅰ	6
bus		8
car	ⅣⅢ ⅣⅢ ⅣⅢ ⅣⅢ ⅠⅠⅠ	
lorry		12
van	ⅣⅢ ⅣⅢ ⅣⅢ	17

(a) Which was the most common vehicle to pass the school? _____

(b) How many vehicles passed the school altogether? _____

2. **A group of boys and girls at an ice rink were asked how old they were. Here are their answers:**

Boys: 8, 10, 10, 11, 9, 8, 8, 9, 10, 11, 8, 8, 10, 8, 9, 10
Girls: 9, 9, 11, 10, 8, 9, 9, 11, 10, 11, 9, 9, 9, 8, 11

Use the charts to make a tally of their answers.

Age	Boys' data
8	
9	
10	
11	

Age	Girls' data
8	
9	
10	
11	

(a) What was the most common age for the boys? _____

(b) Was the most popular age for girls higher or lower than this?

_____

(c) How many students aged 11 were there? _____

Teachers' and parents' note

Give students the opportunity to think of questions that they could answer by collecting data in different ways, for example: Who is tallest? (measuring) What is the most popular colour of car in the car park? (observing) In which month were most students in the class born? (asking) Ask them to design their own collection grids to find the data they need to answer the questions.

Displaying data

Read it!

Key words: bar chart, pictogram, scale, key, title, axes

Data from a tally chart or frequency table can be displayed in a **bar chart** or **pictogram**.

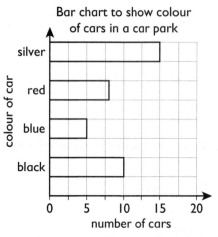

Bar chart to show colour of cars in a car park

Pictogram to show colour of cars in a car park
Key: = 2 cars
black
blue
red
silver

To understand the **scale** on a bar chart, look at what each numbered division stands for.

The **key** on a pictogram shows how much data is represented by one symbol.

Example: Look at the charts above.
Question: How many blue cars were there in the car park?
Answer: 5

Language focus!
Graphs and charts

Block graph	A graph where columns are in blocks. Each block shows 1 item.
Bar chart	A graph where bars are used to show numbers or measurements.
Pictogram	A graph that uses symbols to represent quantities. A key shows what each symbol represents.

Remember that each graph must have a **title** and the **axes** should be labelled to show what the data represents.

6

Think about it!

Look at the bar chart and pictogram about the colour of cars.

(a) Which colour was most popular? _____

(b) How many more black cars were there than blue cars? _____

(c) How many cars were there altogether? _____

Practise it!

1. **Here is a frequency table showing the heights of sunflowers to the nearest 10 cm grown by students in class 4. Use the data to draw the other bars on the bar chart. Add labels and a title to complete the chart.**

Student	Height of sunflower
Ali	60 cm
Erik	120 cm
Luis	70 cm
Igor	90 cm
Ying	100 cm

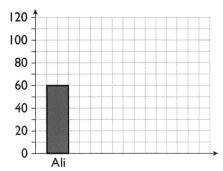

2. **Here is a tally chart to show how many flower bulbs were planted in the school garden.**

Use the data in the tally chart to complete the pictogram.

Pictogram to show the bulbs planted in the school garden.

Type of bulb	Tally
daffodil	⾘⾘⾘ ⾘⾘⾘ ⾘⾘⾘ ⾘⾘⾘ ⾘⾘⾘ ⾘⾘⾘
iris	⾘⾘⾘ ⾘⾘⾘ ⾘⾘⾘
snowdrop	⾘⾘⾘ ⾘⾘⾘ ⾘⾘⾘ ⾘⾘⾘ ⾘⾘⾘
tulip	⾘⾘⾘ ⾘⾘⾘ ⾘⾘⾘ ⾘⾘⾘

Key: ◯ = 10 bulbs
daffodil
iris
snowdrop
tulip

Teachers' and parents' note

Link this activity to the previous unit where the students asked their own questions and collected the data. Allow them to display their data in different ways to see which charts suit which data best.

Comparing data

Read it!

Key words: scale, bar chart, key, pictogram, compare

The **scale** on a **bar chart** or the **key** on a **pictogram** is important when data from two charts is **compared**.

Sometimes the scales on the graphs you are comparing are different and this can be misleading.

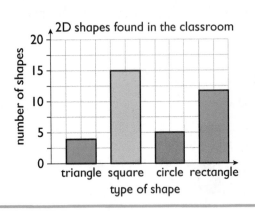

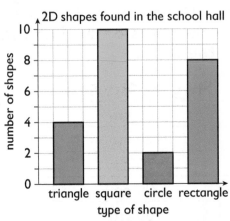

Language focus!

Compare means look for things that are the same or different between two sets of data.

Example: When you compare the two graphs above, you can see that more circles are found in the classroom.

Look carefully at the scale on each graph. The bars in the second graph all look higher but they represent less data as each marker only represents 2 shapes. In the first graph each marker represents 5 shapes.

Think about it!

Look at the graphs above.

(a) How many squares were found in the hall? _____

(b) How many more rectangles were found in the classroom than the hall?

_____

(c) Which shape had an equal number in both the classroom and the hall?

_____

Practise it!

1. **Class 4 run the school snack shop. The graphs show the sales for the last two weeks.**

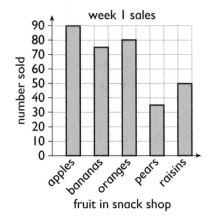

(a) How many bananas did they sell in week 2? _____

(b) Which fruit had the same sales in each week? _____

(c) How many more apples were sold in week 2 than in week 1?
_____

2. **Class 4 drew graphs to show the number of vehicles passing the school in the morning and in the afternoon.**

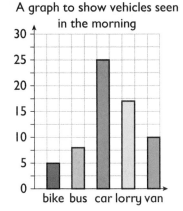

(a) How many bikes did they see in total?

_____

(b) How many more vans were there in the afternoon than the morning? _____

(c) Sally says: "We saw more cars in the afternoon than in the morning."

Is she right? Try to explain your answer. _____

_____

Teachers' and parents' note

Ask students to display the same data on graphs using different scales (or pictograms using different keys) to show how they can be misleading.

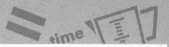

Venn diagrams

Read it!

Key words: Venn diagram, criteria, universal set

A **Venn diagram** is used to show how 2 or 3 sets of data are related to each other.

The sets of data are chosen using properties called **criteria**, for example quadrilaterals or multiples of 3.

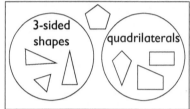

No shapes are in both sets.

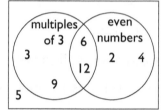

6 and 12 are in both sets.

The number of circles in the Venn diagram relates to the number of criteria being compared. The rectangle represents the **universal set** of all numbers.

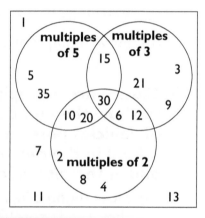

Language focus!

Singular	Plural
property	properties
criterion	criteria

Remember, objects that do not belong in any of the sets are written in the outside box — the universal set.

Think about it!

Look at the Venn diagram for the multiples of 2, 3 and 5.

(a) Which numbers shown are multiples of 2 and 3 only? _____

(b) Which number shown is a multiple of 2, 3 and 5? _____

(c) Write 2 other numbers that would go into the section for the multiples of 2 and 5. _____

Practise it!

1. Here is a Venn diagram for comparing 2D shapes.

Three shapes have been drawn in the wrong places.

Draw arrows from these shapes to show where they should go.

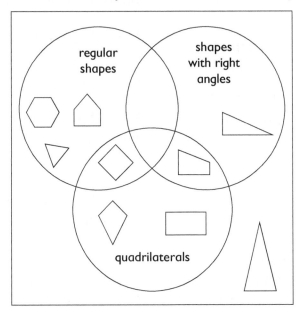

2. Write these numbers in the correct place on the Venn diagram.

6, 7, 8, 9, 10

12, 13, 14, 15

18, 20, 21, 25

30, 60

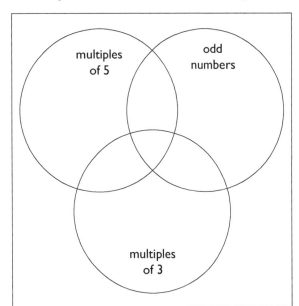

Teachers' and parents' note

Use large hoops with shapes or number cards to represent the different sets and gradually overlap where objects can belong to more than one set. Discuss different ways of deciding on the criteria for sorting the objects.

Key words

Inevitably there are some differences in the vocabulary used internationally. Some key words have alternative versions used in some parts of the world, for example:

Used in this book	Alternative
units	ones
pictogram	pictograph
2D shape	plane shape
3D shape	solid shape
mirror line	line of symmetry

Number

Unit 1 Partitioning numbers
digit, place value, thousand, zero, place value holder, partition, ten thousand (10 000)

Unit 2 Decimal numbers
decimal, decimal point, tenth, hundredth, decimal place

Unit 3 Rounding numbers
round (a number to …), between (half way between), closer to, closest to

Unit 4 Comparing numbers
compare, size, number line, order, greater than (>), less than (<)

Unit 5 Negative numbers
negative number, positive number, zero, temperature

Unit 6 Odd and even numbers
even, odd, next, general statement, counter example

Unit 7 Number sequences
sequence, rule, term continue, count on, count back

Unit 8 Equivalent fractions
equivalent fraction, numerator, denominator, part (equal parts)

Unit 9 Ordering fractions
compare, numerator, order, denominator, number line

Unit 10 Mixed numbers
mixed number, order, compare, number line

Unit 11 Addition
calculate, add, plus, sum, more than, total, number line, partition

Unit 12 Subtraction
subtract, minus, difference, take away, count back, leave (left)

Unit 13 Multiplication and division
multiple, inverse

Unit 14 Mental strategies
recall, derive, pairs, total

Unit 15 Multiplication
product, multiply, grid method, times

Unit 16 Division
divide by, divide into, share, remainder, half (halve)

Unit 17 Division problems
context, round up, round down

Geometry

Unit 18 Polygons
polygon, quadrilateral, pentagon, hexagon, heptagon, octagon, regular, irregular

Unit 19 Quadrilaterals
2-dimensional, quadrilateral, side, vertex (vertices), square, rectangle, kite, adjacent, opposite, pinboard

Unit 20 Symmetrical shapes
symmetrical, line of symmetry, reflection, mirror line, polygon, regular

Unit 21 3D shapes
3-dimensional, solid, cuboid, prism, pyramid, tetrahedron, face, edge, vertex, base, cube

Unit 22 Nets
net, pyramid, prism, cuboid

Unit 23 Using grids
grid, row, column, horizontal, vertical, axis (axes), position

Unit 24 Giving directions
directions, left, right, up, down, route

Unit 25 Angles
angle, degree, right angle, clockwise, anticlockwise

Measures

Unit 26 Length
kilometres, metres, centimetres, millimetres

Unit 27 Capacity and mass
litres, millilitres, grams, kilograms

Unit 28 12-hour clock
day, hour, minute, second, midnight, noon, analogue clock, digital clock

Unit 29 Timetables
timetable, arrive, depart, calendar, date

Unit 30 Perimeter
perimeter, length, width

Unit 31 Area
area, square centimetre, square metre

Data handling

Unit 32 Using tables
table, row, column, Carroll diagram, sort

Unit 33 Collecting data
data, tally chart, frequency table, tally marks

Unit 34 Displaying data
bar chart, pictogram, scale, key, title, axes

Unit 35 Comparing data
scale, bar chart, key, pictogram, compare

Unit 36 Venn diagrams
Venn diagram, criteria, universal set

Notes